The Sea Otter's Struggle

The Sea Otter's Struggle

JANE H. BAILEY

Foreword by Judson E. Vandevere
Hopkins Marine Station, Stanford University

 **Follett Publishing Company**
Chicago

Cp 1

Photo Credits

Jane H. Bailey: *page 46*. Bureau of Sport Fisheries and Wildlife, United States Department of the Interior/Karl W. Kenyon: *pages 27, 49, 51, 69, 78*. State of California, Department of Parks and Recreation: *page 60*. E. E. Ebert: California Department of Fish and Game, Marine Research Division: *pages 39, 40*. Franklin Enos: *page 34*. Karl W. Kenyon: *pages 16, 30, 33, 53, 55, 59, 66, 70, 74, 76, 91*. Roger and Joy Spur: *cover, pages 20-21, 81, 83, 84*.

Library of Congress Catalog Card Number: 72-85578
ISBN 0-695-80373-5 Trade binding
ISBN 0-695-40373-7 Titan binding
First Printing

4 |

Contents

Foreword   *7*

One   **Introduction**   *11*

Two   **Meet the Sea Otter**   *13*

Three   **The Sea Otter Close-up**   *18*

Four   **An Intelligent Animal**   *24*

Five   **Early Life of the Pup**   *29*

Six   **The Otter Habitat**   *37*

Seven   **Discovery of the Furry Crescent and the Fur Stampede**   *44*

Eight   **The Great Hunt and the Native Aleut**   *50*

Nine   **Last Years of the Great Hunt**   *57*

Ten   **Evolution and Survival**   *64*

Eleven   **To See an Otter**   *72*

Twelve   **An Otter Safari**   *80*

Thirteen   **Otter Enemies**   *87*

Reference List   *93*

Foreword

THE SEA OTTER, the lovable subject of this fine book, is the most recent mammal to become wholly marine, is the only subprimate tool-using mammal, and is the smallest of the marine mammals. This inshore predator performs a needed biological control by preventing population explosions of urchins and other inhibitors of kelp growth.

An ever-widening public has taken up otter watching as an exciting and satisfying experience. Nowhere on earth are sea otters more easily viewed than on the Monterey Peninsula of Central California. Here, groups of up to one hundred forty sea otters may be observed living close together in peaceful coexistence, an amazing feat for members of the weasel family.

Although, historically, sea otters have avoided leaving the water along continental shores where they were easy prey to large predators like grizzly bears and humans, in recent months a half-dozen or more otters have been seen hauling out in the Monterey area. Some have been tamed by divers and are now becoming sufficiently bold to handle the divers' face masks or remove their mouthpieces.

Jane Bailey has done an excellent reference job, obtaining the latest information from reliable studies. THE SEA OTTER'S STRUGGLE encompasses much of the known facts concerning one of the earth's most fascinating creatures.

Judson E. Vandevere
Hopkins Marine Station
Stanford University
June 1973

The Sea Otter's Struggle

One

Introduction

OUR world may have been truly discovered in 1969 when man first viewed his planet from outer space and realized that it is self-contained. Perhaps this discovery also shows that people need to co-operate in caring for their ecosystem, the life-support system for the human species.

Ecology is the relationship between organisms and their environment. *Eco* is the Greek word for house. The world is our house, and that includes the surrounding envelope several hundred feet thick called the biosphere where plant and animal life can thrive.

No longer can people dump waste material into rivers or seas without conscience. Nor can people scatter waste into the air from bomb-testing, combustion engines, or paper mill vats. Water and air are not curbed by frontier borders but find their way to other lands and other branches of the family of man.

Each link in the chain of life is important in keeping the earth healthy, and the sea otter is one link. The threat to his existence has moved a considerable number of people to act individually and cooperatively to protect the ecosystem and to insure the sea otter's survival.

Conservationists may one day call 1969 the year of the sea otter as well as the year that man discovered his world.

Two

Meet the Sea Otter

THE sea otter lives in water, but his skin never gets wet. He is born in the sea but must learn to swim. Although he is a carnivore, his food comes only from the sea.

Enhydra lutris is the scientific name of this animal. He is not a close relative to man yet his behavior is often tender—almost human. This is one of the things that fascinates people and makes them want to learn as much as possible about the sea otter's life style and history.

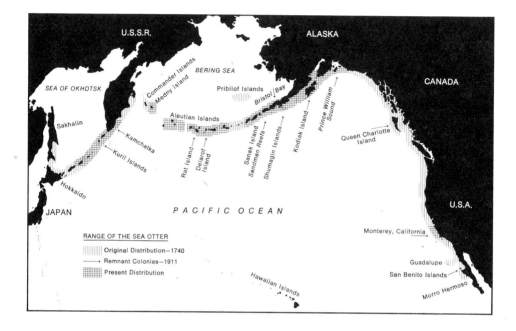

The otter's inventiveness and his devotion to his own species are shown in the lengthy, careful training period which is given to the young. However, it is just plain fun to observe the happy nature of the sea otter.

From the coast of Japan, up through the Kurile Islands and the Russian Commander Islands, east across the Aleutian Islands, down the coasts of Alaska, Canada, Oregon, Washington, and California, to Mexico's peninsula called Baja California, once stretched the range of this valuable furbearer.

Nowhere else in the world except in this "furry crescent" was he reported in existence. Scientists think he was once a land or river animal that went to sea two million years ago in Asia.

Today most of the world's otters live in the shallow waters of Alaska and the many Aleutian Islands. In 1965 about 26,000 were in this area. The Russian Commander Islands had approximately 1,000, and another thousand lived in the warmer waters along the coast of California.

The scientist who has examined the most skeletal material believes there is a slight difference in species between the northern and southern sea otters. Their life styles and their diets also differ a little. The Alaskan otter often goes ashore to groom himself and to seek shelter from stormy seas. But it is a rare occasion when a California otter goes ashore. He is born, lives, and dies in the ocean—a half mile to a mile offshore. The northern otters at Amchitka, in the Aleutian Islands, eat much fish, perhaps 50 percent of their food intake, and the rest shellfish. The southerners eat practically no fish, for their diet consists of clams, crabs, mussels, squid, abalone, octopus, and urchins.

Unfortunately, few humans have been privileged to see the otter's way of life at first hand. The cruelties of the great otter hunt of the 1700s and 1800s, described in Chapters 7, 8, and 9, drove him to live as far from man as he could. By 1911 these seagoing weasels were close to extinction.

Sea otters live in large groups called rafts. The raft may
contain over a hundred animals, as shown in this aerial view
of a raft.

The otters that lived in the Alaskan waters recovered with the help of International and United States' laws against destruction. The otter that lived along the coast of California was also protected by these laws as well as by California laws, but this species barely recovered beyond the endangered stage. Nowadays polluted waters and boat propellers threaten the southern sea otters.

The sea otter leads a life high in drama. The small mammal has had to cope with starvation, animal competition, predators, and human enemies. Even so, otter families happily play and work through their days, and, under man's protection, they gradually increase their numbers.

Three

The Sea Otter Close-up

WHAT brought the sea otter to near extinction was his fur—dense, deep, chocolate brown, and silky. It has been called the diamond among furs, so handsome and fine are the fibers. The inch-long fur has 650,000 hairs per square inch. There are 800,000,000 hairs on a single five or six foot animal. The prized fur seal has only half this much fur.

The fur varies from brown to nearly black, and that of the underside is occasionally lighter in color than that which is on the back. The winter pelt is not noticeably darker than summer's. The pup is born with shaggy, yellowish fur which is longer than that of his parents. He looks disheveled although his mother grooms and preens his fur throughout the day. The odd-looking coat serves as a life jacket to keep him on the water's surface while his mother dives for food.

The otter is a high-floating creature who appears coated with gelatin or dipped in chocolate. His luxurious fur has unique qualities for keeping his skin dry; only the tips get wet. They cling to form a thin outer layer which wards off water.

Inside this dense coat is up to 70 pounds of female otter or up to 100 pounds of male otter. A newborn otter weighs from four to five pounds and may be as long as two feet. An adult otter is usually four or four and one-half feet long.

This animal has a little ball of a head with black eyes that sparkle and pointed ears which close automatically when he dives. Some baby otters have a gray face and head like an old-timer; thus a youngster can have face fur to match his grandfather's. The otter's nose is diamond-shaped and flat giving his muzzle a blunt appearance.

Crisp, bristly whiskers spray downward like a Chinese mandarin's beard. Generally their length is a couple of inches, worn down from serving as antennae to guide the otter among sea-bottom rocks or on stony beaches. When an otter is in captivity, his whiskers can reach four inches.

More than half of the otter's 32 teeth are flat

Sea otters usually float and swim on their backs, whether eating, sleeping, resting, or grooming. They often rest with both forepaws on cheek or chest.

molars and postcanines used for grinding shellfish and not for chewing or tearing meat. The teeth of the old otters may become eroded because their favorite foods are shellfish.

The otter has several tones of voice and each has a clear meaning, even to the few men who have had experience with him. A baby's cry is sharp, shrill, like a young sea gull. An adult's distress scream protests the kidnaping or killing of a pup and can be heard up to a half mile. A whine or

whistle indicates frustration, as shown when a mother is tardy at feeding time. Cooing is for courtship between adults, but it also soothes the young while mothers roughly groom their fur with teeth and toenails. If food is satisfactory, otters grunt. Hissing seems to be either a warning or an expression of fright. A newly captured otter growls. Some people have described another sound as the penny-whistle tone.

The sea otter can catch the scent of a campfire

four or five miles away. His sense of touch is unusual, too, as shown by the use of his paws for affectionate caressing.

Often an otter lies resting with his forepaws on his cheek or chest. If the sun shines in his eyes, he can shade them with his forepaws. The paws have claws that function like fingers to comb fur or pull clams and snails from the sea bottom and mussels from a reef.

Loose skin forms a pouch when the otter holds one foreleg against its chest. An otter visiting a fish and wildlife station in the Aleutians demonstrated the use of her saggy skin as a market basket. Encouraged by scientists, the otter came on shore for a handout. She stuffed 18 two-inch clams into her pouch. Number 19 was too much, and most of her clams fell to the ground. The greedy otter pressed the food cache of eight clams to her belly and shuffled off to the sea on three legs. When last seen, she was floating with belly and clams skyward while leisurely dining.

The otter's hind flippers are broad, flat, and fanlike. They hamper progress over the black, volcanic rubble of the Aleutian Island beaches but are handy in a sea sprint. His tail, which resembles a piece of flattened gardenhose, serves as an oar. Because forelegs do not help in locomotion, his travel is slow. He moves leisurely while lying on his back but can attain a speed of about four miles per hour while swimming on his abdomen.

Besides floating on his back and swimming on

either his back or his stomach, the sea otter is often upright in the water. When humans approach, he may stand high for a better view. A female will stand, holding her pup by his shoulders out in front of her as though teaching him to tread water.

The rib cage of the sea otter measures two-thirds of his total length, including the tail. This helps protect him from the constant pounding of the waves.

Four
An Intelligent Animal

THE otter uses his wits to make his work easier. He is the only subprimate mammal for which reliable observations have been made of tool-use.

Using a double-fist-sized rock as an anvil, the California sea otter lays it on his chest and fractures shellfish against it. There is no evidence that the Alaskan otter uses the anvil, but not many large shellfish live in this area. Besides, his diet is 50 percent fish. Some captive Alaskan otters strike one shellfish against another to reach the meat inside.

An American authority on the sea otter, Karl Kenyon of the U.S. Bureau of Sport Fisheries and Wildlife, suggests that the rock pounding may have begun when disappointment drove an otter to express this emotion by breast beating. He saw one otter, who was robbed by another of his food, beat his breast. Perhaps the nonaggressive otter expresses his frustration this way rather than in fighting.

The rock hammer is also used to weaken the strong grip of an abalone mollusk on the rocky sea bottom. Abalone divers have found many shells with a hole in the center throughout the area inhabited by abalone and sea otter. Because it takes three to five hundred pounds of leverage to pry an abalone from its mooring, sea otters would have to devise some means of removing the meat.

Cleaning and grooming methods are creative. Sometimes all four feet work at once combing and scrubbing. The otter's loose skin and long rib cage make it easy for him to squirm and bend in reaching all areas of his coat. So flexible is his body that he can spin his torso around as he lies on his back and still keep his head and flippers clear of the water. Frequent whirling and rolling in the surf is not just in play; this removes food scraps and slime from his fur. Since the otter's life depends upon a clean suit, he instinctively tidies up even between bites.

To aerate his fur to maintain an air blanket, the otter lies face down on the surface of the water. He tucks his head under his chest like a chicken or bird and blows air into the fur, at the same time buffing his side fur with his paws. Sometimes he churns up a cloud of bubbles by thrashing the water all around him with his forepaws.

Another means by which the sea otter uses his own physical traits to his best advantage is noted in his method of securing sea urchins from the bottom of the ocean. These red and purple balls, which resemble an explosion, are carried when small in a temporary chest pouch. He can then lie in his watery hammock and munch his urchin lunch, plucking the creatures one by one from his pouch.

The sea otter also is the only animal known to use kelp strands as anchors. He drapes them over his body to anchor it in the kelp beds. This helps to keep him from drifting while taking his siesta.

An early visitor to Alaska observed an otter lobbing a baseball-sized kelp bladder from one paw to the other before letting it fall into the sea. Recently a busload of tourists reportedly enjoyed watching two California otters as they continuously passed an old hubcap from one to the other.

One captive otter struck chunks of coralline algae one against the other. Another captive chipped at the edge of his pool with rocks left within his reach. The drain at the bottom of an otter pool in the Seattle zoo was covered by fitted wire mesh. The lone otter removed the wire so often that its keepers covered the drain with a sturdy screen reinforced with a metal band and bolted it down. The little otter pounded the new cover with a rock until it, too, gave way.

The gray or white face on an adult otter is usually an indication of age, but not always. Males usually have lighter facial fur than females.

Invention is not the only evidence of the otter's intelligence. His consideration and concern for his own species is unusual. Because the otter sometimes demonstrates responsibility, affection, and humor, it is easy to consider him a notch above most creatures.

For example, a captive male threw himself over two females, believing he was protecting them from their keeper. It is difficult to imagine a sea lion doing such a thing—or waking his mate when a human approaches to warn her to head for the sea, as the otter has done.

In the north competition for food comes from other otters, seals, sea lions, and river otters. River otters compete with sea otters for shellfish, even though they are not marine mammals. Yet, there are no reported clashes over the food.

Divers have seen an occasional fight between otters, but squabbles have never been reported when different animals seek out the same spot on a beach. A harbor seal will nudge an otter from his own accustomed resting place on the rocks, but when the tables are turned, the otter does not react the same way. His disposition allows a dripping relative to use him as a beach towel even when he has just finished drying and grooming his own fur.

Sea otters seldom become annoyed by each other. Even in captivity feeding hours have brought almost no collisions. Once an otter snatched another's supper. The loser was true to character; he was not even irritated.

Sea otters are not likely to meet death from their own kind. They are especially gentle and nonaggressive because nature provides for their needs.

Russian biologists found that a captive otter responds to fondling and caressing. When they freed a captive after four months, he refused to leave and stayed two more weeks before returning to the sea.

Five

Early Life of the Pup

THE sea otter has a long childhood. He spends most of his first months floating on his mother's abdomen; for almost a year he remains dependent on her. Nature gives the mother otter only one pup at a time, and the period between births is about two years. Practically never is a young otter seen at his mother's side while she is serving as raft and teacher for his baby brother or sister.

Scientists believe that the length of an animal's

The baby otter spends most of its first year being carried on its mother's chest. The pup also will rest there when it is nursing. Only one pup is born at a time, and usually one is born every two years.

training period corresponds with the intelligence of his species. *Enhydra lutris* rates high in intelligence although there has not been enough opportunity for controlled experiments of the species.

People who live near the central California coast have formed an organization called Friends of the Sea Otter. They spend many hours otter-watching through binoculars or 20-power scopes. They log their observations and keep a file of still and motion pictures.

When an otter is born, the observers say the mother places the small puff on her chest. For nine days she feeds only her infant. At mealtime she lifts him high off her chest with her forepaws, slowly turns him about, and then lowers him head first to her body for breast-feeding. Afterward, she reverses him again, carefully, so that he will not get wet. When the mother finally eats, she may take only a few legs of a kelp crab and stow the rest of the creature in her pouch.

The observers say that the mother otter frequently licks and grooms the pup, but she gives her own coat only an occasional hasty swipe. Sometimes she gently lays the pup on the water's surface and turns a few quick cartwheels, probably to clean her coat. Then she dives and comes up beneath the pup so that he is again resting on her abdomen with his head under her chin.

The Aleutian Islands' pup is probably born on land among the rocks and stones which line the sea. His mother brings him to shore daily for breast-feeding, a scrub-down, and a nap. After a few weeks of helplessness, the pup begins to crawl and swim in an uncoordinated fashion.

The mother carries her infant on her abdomen to a quiet pool for his swimming lessons. By sinking from beneath him, she leaves the pup afloat like a wisp of down. Most of his day is spent trying to imitate his mother, who teaches him to swim by moving a little further from him with every lesson. He cannot dive because of the buoyancy of his shaggy fur. His head may dip under, but then his back muscles are too weak to lift his head from the water. So, he rolls over, belly up.

The mother otter plays happily with her pup, caressing him, all the while keeping him dry. She uses her teeth and forepaws to pull him from the water and replaces him on her abdomen. With all her affection and close attention, the mother otter is firm as she trains her pup. Young otters submit to the rules. They accept the rigorous grooming process, though they cry out from the rough handling. Bouncing like rag dolls, the newborn pups let themselves be dragged across the rocky shores of the islands.

Old otters are gentle and good-natured toward the lively youngsters. During naptime when young and old, male and female are floating peacefully in a kelp bed, the little ones occasionally frolick. They shoot up from the sea like missiles onto the stomach of one of their elders who has stretched out for a few winks. The grandfather otter allows the youngsters to enjoy this game without so much as boxing their ears, nipping, or snapping. It is a mother who finally halts the play by calling her offspring, if she cannot see him, and obediently he comes to her.

The mother otter is very devoted. Even after the

The mother sea otter is very devoted. After she finishes preening her own fur, she preens her pup's fur and then allows the pup to nurse.

pup can swim on his back like an adult, the mother allows him to hitchhike on her abdomen. If something startles her, she grasps her pup in one arm and swims rapidly away. When thoroughly frightened, she may make an escape dive with her pup gripped between her teeth. If her pup dies, she mourns for days, carrying the body with her.

An Amchitka Island pup wandered out of his mother's sight as they rested on the shore. After

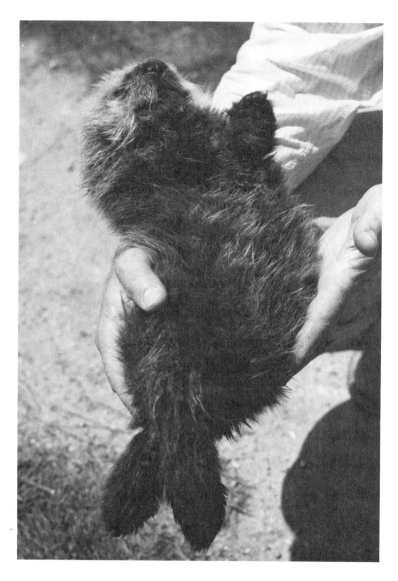

This rescued sea otter pup was washed ashore near
Monterey, California. After a night of being cared for by
humans, it was returned to the sea and to its mother.

a few minutes she discovered the disappearance
and hurried off to look for him. Like a human
mother and child, they were almost hysterical before they finally found each other. However, the
adventure ended with demonstrations of joy from
both.

Recently a storm tossed a young otter ashore near
Monterey, California. Nearby residents heard the
pup's cries and rescued it. Out beyond the noisy
surf they were unable to see the mother.

The pup spent a warm, dry and comfortable night
with the young son of a naturalist who bottle-fed
the otter a formula of whipping cream and baby-
food. Next morning, despite the continuing rough
surf, a pair of scuba divers lashed a wire basket
to a surfboard, placed the pup in it, and slid out to
the kelp beds. Here they deposited the crying baby
on a thick mesh of seaweed. The men backpaddled
a short distance and then waited until they saw
the mother sprint toward her offspring.

At an observation station on Amchitka Island a
friendly relationship developed between the men
and two otters. But this relationship cooled because of the mother otter's anxiety for her pup.
The two otters had visited from time to time, even
eating from the hands of the men. Then one day
the men decided the friendship was close enough
to allow them to pick up the pup and weigh it. The
mother dropped her snack, screamed, stood on
her hind legs, and beat against the man holding the
pup until he released it.

Hunters learned that the mother continues to defend her young to the end. At the first alarm, she and the pup are likely to clutch each other with their forearms. The mother may even bite the human. When she sees there is no more she can do, she may cradle the pup in her arms and turn her back on the enemy, accepting defeat.

Male and female otters stay together for a period during courtship, but observers believe they do not remain as a family. However, a group of otters separated into nurseries, remains together as a unit for a time. Otters do not migrate; however, when a pup matures, he may leave the pod.

Six

The Otter Habitat

A valuable otter friend is the seaweed, kelp. These giant algae provide him with a network of heavy stems and fronds for camouflage and protective coloring.

Of the two similar varieties of kelp—giant and bull—which grow along the coast, the bull has the coloring and the texture that somewhat resembles the fur and flippers of the otter. Even the bull's brown bladders grow almost as large as an otter's head. It should be no surprise that the otter made this alga's habitat his own.

The giant's massive tangles of stipes, bladders, and blades grow up to 151 feet tall and can spread its fronds thickly enough to hold boats at bay. The stipes and blades even help quiet the waters churned up by wind or tide, which might otherwise buffet the otter and dash him against rocks and reefs. In some places the rangy kelp is dense enough to support a pup when a mother sets him down on a snarl of it. Here also is her tool, the frond, which she drapes over the pup to keep him from drifting. Kelp seems an all-purpose friend, also providing nourishment for two of the otter's foods, the sea urchin and the abalone. If the four organisms live together in a healthy balance, it also helps man. The urchin and the abalone feed on kelp; the otter feeds on both of them.

By eating the urchin the otter controls the urchin population, thus leaving ample kelp for himself, for the abalone, and for man.

People use kelp in many ways. Its harvest brings algin to make ice cream smoother, mayonnaise thicker, car polish creamier, and finger paints and toothpaste pastier. Not only do many products contain this algin, but kelp itself may soon be an important source of food instead of simply an additive.

If allowed to thrive, purple and red urchins can form a massive parade of about 100 per square yard, daily advancing several feet through kelp planta-

The sea urchin is one of the most essential foods in the sea otter's diet. The sea otter crushes the urchin with his teeth or opens it with his paws. Then he scoops out and eats the contents.

This abalone shellfish is eating a kelp seaweed stem. The abalone is one of the major food sources for the sea otter.

tions. Urchins can sever the short rootlike growth of the holdfast which clings to the bottom rock. The kelp's anchorage is weakened so that during heavy swells the plants are torn loose.

Recently in one southern California area the urchin population went out of control and mowed down the kelp. (There have been no otters in this area for many years.) The abalone's downfall followed the kelp's. Some members of the abalone fishing industry wanted otters herded to areas where they could control the balance of urchin, kelp, and abalone.

The otter's healthy appetite encourages him to compete with commercial and sports fishermen for the abalone. One eight-and-one-quarter-inch abalone weighing two and three-tenths pounds without the shell equals 63 of his favorite small mussels, 31 small purple urchins, two large gaper clams, or three red urchins. It would take 270 small purple urchins to equal the 13 pounds of food that an adult otter needs daily. Thus catching one abalone saves many dives for enough sea cucumbers, mussels, scallops, chitons, tubeworms, clams or crabs to satisfy his appetite.

Among an otter's secrets is how he loosens the abalone's clutch, since it is a difficult job for a man. Abalone divers spent many years trying to convince people that the little five-foot animal with short forelegs and tiny paws could pit his strength against the pull of three to five hundred pounds of abalone grip.

The otter has not been caught in the act because he streaks away when a human comes near. But there are many abalone shells with identical holes in them lying near the abalone beds where otters live. Biologists have explained that the otter uses his rock anvil for pounding a hole in the coarse shell. The stunned abalone then loosens its grip.

During the 1960s some young male California otters drifted a few miles south of the refuge that had been created to protect them, to some beds of red abalone. Perhaps there was not enough food for the growing otter population in their former refuge. By 1969 almost two dozen animals were using the beds which had long been part of the abalone industry.

The commercial fishermen who had harvested these red abalone beds for many years were convinced that the abalone must be rescued from the hungry otters. Sportsmen who dived for abalone were also alarmed that the animals were using these beds.

Unfortunately, both otters and many people eat all sizes of abalone, including those too young to have spawned. Law-abiding fishermen, however, take only large legal-sized abalone—those old enough to have spawned.

Although few people may have eaten the white, solid, and sweet flesh of the abalone, many know its handsome rainbow shell. The red abalone has an oval bowl that can exceed eleven inches in diameter. Craftsmen make art objects and jewelry from the heavy shell. They first polish its rough exterior, which is covered with tubeworm casings, barnacles, and weeds which camouflages the mollusk from divers and other predators. Because of the abalone's tight grip, the easiest way for a man to remove it is with a crowbar or a tire iron.

Seven

Discovery of the
Furry Crescent
and the Fur Stampede

IN the mid-1700s Russia's Czar Peter the Great was curious about the physical world and its peoples. He hired Vitus Bering, a Danish navigator, to sail from Siberia northward between the continents of Asia and America to see if they were joined at any point.

The European white men were ignorant of these lands, their inhabitants, and the plant and animal life that were peculiar to the area. The first to describe them was Georg Steller, the German scien-

tist who accompanied Bering. He used sketches
and the written word to report his explorations
and discoveries.

Bering found water separating Asia and America; he also discovered the Aleutian and the Commander Islands. On his last voyage home he was
shipwrecked on one of the Commanders, which
was later named Bering Island. Although he and
many of his crew did not survive long, those who
did were starving until they accidentally found sea
otters resting on a beach. Here was food as well as
fur for protection against the cold. Before the men
left the island, they collected two hundred of the
rich otter fur pelts.

Before this time, north Pacific storms had sometimes swept sea otters onto beaches of the Kam-
chatka peninsula of Sibera. Lucky hunters had become wealthy selling the precious fur for royal
garments. But no one had found the otter habitat.

When the remnants of Bering's crew returned to
Siberia in their homemade boat, they knew where
the otter lived. And in Canton, China, across the
Russian frontier, they found a fabulous fur market
—this touched off the fur rush.

If the Europeans had been less greedy and more
reasonable in hunting the sea otter, they would
not have endangered the species. As it was, they
brought it to near extinction. The total haul during
the 170-year hunt has been estimated as between
one-half and one million otters.

In their haste to get to the fur fields, many Siberian hunters went out to sea in poorly built

A rare otter pelt is displayed in California's Indian Museum in Sacramento. The dense, luxurious fur is called the diamond among furs. Large and saggy, the pelt may stretch to nearly six feet long.

ships which easily crashed against the reefs. These wandering outcasts were accustomed to driving themselves hard. With recklessness and courage they resorted to ramshackle boats nicknamed *skitiki,* meaning sewed or stitched. Poorly cut and unseasoned timbers were hurriedly lashed together with leather thongs because no metal or nails were available.

The white man was responsible for the death of five thousand otters the first year he arrived in the little Pribilof Islands, north of the Aleutian Islands. In the second year less than one thousand otters remained and in the sixth not one could be found among all the Pribilofs.

Spain dominated what is now California and Baja California as well as Mexico, Central America, and South America. Before she colonized the California regions, her explorers were sailing along the coast and trading with the natives, who knew the otter well. The mammal populated the shores of the Californias and their offshore islands like a "thick black fringe." Before 1800 Spain had sold ten thousand otter pelts in China.

Otter fur was already fashionable as capes, belts, and pearl-trimmed borders for the robes of wealthy Chinese by the time Russians and other Europeans discovered its beauty and warmth. Spanish ships, called Manila galleons, traded between Mexico and the Orient, transporting the furs via the Philippine Islands to China. The first otter pelt that arrived in the Orient may have been a wrapper for a package. If so, a Manila galleon was probably the carrier.

During the first half century of the great hunt, the United States was still a small cluster of colonies on the east coast of the North American continent. England's Captain James Cook discovered the otter trade during one of his voyages and carried the news to New England clipper ship captains. These were enterprising seafarers who ranged all over the globe whaling and trading a wide assortment of cargo. Most of these ships and their skippers came from Boston, and they were called Boston captains or Yankee skippers by the rest of the world.

Portugal, France, and Great Britain were all well represented at the fur stampede. Their citizens had been attracted by the news that an early Russian hunter earned a half million dollars in the sea otter fur trade.

During the otter hunt of the 1700s, sea otters were afraid of humans from puppyhood on. Since the otters have been protected by law, they seem to be less afraid. Here, a native Alaskan has made friends with two unwary pups.

Eight

The Great Hunt
and the Native Aleut

INSTINCT drives one animal to prey upon another
for survival. Primitive people preyed upon animals
too, for food, clothing, and shelter. Yet they understood nature's ways well enough to conserve wildlife for their future needs by not overkilling.

Nature provided the Aleuts with the necessities
for survival. The land offered vegetation for food,
clothing, and shelter. The seas were a cornucopia
of meat, vegetables, and seafood. Portions of the
whale and sea lion provided waterproof, windproof
clothing.

During World War II, many servicemen described sea otters as "goofy little animals playing offshore." Several members of this Aleutian raft are alert to observers, but they also are well camouflaged as they float among the kelp fronds and bladders.

As early as 2000 B.C. the Aleuts had their complex culture. They may have arrived in the Western Hemisphere in 6000 B.C. Their kayak was made of sea lion hide which needed little care more than an occasional docking to dry it out. It was thistle-light, and could be carried with one hand. The craft was about twenty-one feet long and only two feet wide. Its slender frames were fashioned of driftwood, because very little timber grew on the tundra of the islands.

When a native of the Aleutian Islands wriggled into his snug, cork-light kayak to go otter hunting, he checked his amulet before reaching for his double paddle. This charm was made of stone or bone, and fashioned into the likeness of the quarry. Its purpose was to reduce the otter's cunning.

Skilled and brave hunters were almost worshipped. But it was not the otter which earned these men the highest honors among their people. It was the whale. This was the creature demanding the most in art and courage from a man who would capture it.

By the time the white man arrived, thirty thousand Aleuts had gathered a storehouse of knowledge regarding the anatomy of the mammals in the waters around them. They had used intelligence and energy to outwit the whale, sea lion, and otter, but had had no need to outwit other humans.

Those untamed adventurers, the *promyshlenniki*, took advantage of the Aleuts. They would order the natives to deliver a specific number of furs, and the penalty for not meeting the demand could mean many deaths or the burning of an entire village. Using methods such as holding Aleut youngsters and wives as hostages, hunters forced the men to pursue the otter. The "magic" bullet was also effective in controlling the Aleuts, because the natives believed the bullet would chase them no matter in which direction they ran.

The tragedy of the great hunt was that the white

In water the sea otter is a nimble creature, but on land, the sea otter walks with a very clumsy gait.

man used both innocent creatures, native Aleut and otter, with little conscience. Few tribes could resist the determined Russian hunters who destroyed the peaceful life of these primitive and gentle people.

It was 40 years before the Siberian hunters became fur company employees. The fur companies improved the relations between the natives and the trappers. Russia's czarina even took notice of the inhumane practices against the Aleuts and insisted on less harsh treatment toward them.

However, her charity came too late because thousands of Aleuts had already been lost since the white man's arrival.

The Aleuts were so terrified of their white oppressors that they struggled to meet the fur quotas. Often they banded together in a flotilla of one or two hundred kayaks. The first hunter to sight an otter raised his paddle to signal the others. Forming a circle they closed like a drawstring around their prey.

When the otter saw these humans approach, he dived into the water. When he surfaced for oxygen, the closest hunter screamed and threw his harpoon. If the weapon missed its mark, the otter would quickly dive again—often without time to fill his lungs. Eventually this procedure of repeated dives and too little oxygen exhausted the otter. The prize went to the hunter whose harpoon lodged nearest the victim's head.

Aleuts have reported that the otter's escape dive lasted from 5 to 15 minutes. Yet, according to authorities, 5 minutes is a prolonged dive. The ordinary dive for food lasts 50 or 60 seconds in water less than 60 feet deep. The California otter's maximum depth is about 100 feet, and the Alaskan's is 200.

Despite his sharp wits, the otter was handicapped during the great hunt. He had neither speed nor a refuge. He was forced to devise a number of tricks to postpone his death. One trick was to slip under the kayak beyond reach of the har-

When the sea otter is cornered on land and its escape route is blocked, it lies on its back and stiffens and extends its forelegs. If the sea otter is touched, it may try biting and pushing the intruder.

poon in a serious game of hide-and-seek. Another trick was to streak shoreward toward the rip current created by "piled up" water inside sandbars. Here a powerful sweep of tide flows back into the sea. A rip current could upset the Aleut's almost un-upsettable craft. Sometimes the otter hid himself in a sea cave. When the tide was ebbing, this crevice in a reef was open to the air, allowing the otter to breathe. If a net was tossed over the cave mouth until the incoming tide filled the space, the otter drowned.

Early in the great hunt, a campfire attracted the sea mammal. Soon he refused to approach even an old campsite four or five miles away. The scent of human litter could throw the otter into a panic, and he learned to leave the shore when he caught the smell of man's footprints in the sand or pebbles. Until the tide had come in time and time again, the otter avoided those beaches.

Hunters admired the intelligence of the otters. One wrote, "Them otter have a human sense." Adult otters seemed to pass their terror of humans to even their youngest pups.

The plunderers learned to take advantage of mother love and instinct to swell their harvest of pelts. Squeezing a pup until it whimpered or wailed attracted the mother. Leaving a pup on the beach or on seaweed matting in the sea surrounded by stout fishhooks often trapped adults. An occasional tug on the line was enough to snag the otter that answered the pup's distress signals.

Georg Steller, who accompanied Vitus Bering's voyage, explained the reason for the hunters' success. He wrote of the otter, "Their love for their young is so intense that for them they expose themselves to the most manifest danger of death."

Nine

Last Years of the Great Hunt

THE fur stampede was in full swing under the Russian American Company by 1800. This company was the official arm of the Russian government in America. The first director of this fur company was Aleksandr Andreevich Baranov, who was the complete master and governor of Russian interests on the North American continent for many years.

The strong-willed director controlled the Aleut and the Kodiak tribes through his Siberian employees. These men were not as deeply enslaved as the Aleuts, yet they were dependent on Baranov, subject to all of his whims or plots.

As soon as Baranov arrived in America, he recognized the overharvesting of the otter population. Since the time of Captain Cook's voyage when the otter's value was understood by Europeans and Americans, the competition in fur fields had cut into the Russian hunting monopoly. So Baranov used unreasonable means to get furs.

He sent out expeditions under inhumane conditions. Hundreds of two-men kayaks hunted as far as a thousand miles from home. They paddled hour after hour without rest.

Harpooned otters were skinned along the way to the hunting grounds. One man leaned over the gunwhale to do the work while the other held the kayak steady. If a killer whale caught the scent or taste of the otter, he could upset the kayak. The natives got no campfire for comfort or for hot food and drink because the smell of smoke might have panicked the otter and driven him away. In this instance, the Russian masters also suffered, but they, too, had to return to Sitka with the quota of pelts ordered by Baranov.

Although the Aleut and other native cultures buckled under the force of the white man, the Tlingits of the mainland (near Sitka) resisted the Russian hunters indefinitely. This tribe of fishermen was known for its magnificent totems, canoes, great houses of wood, and beautifully designed blankets woven from the mountain goat's wool.

When sea otters move quickly (less than the running speed of a human), they move their forepaws and hind feet in a hopping manner.

Their descendants continue today to follow the salmon, but under modern conditions.

The Tlingits massacred the first Russian colony at Sitka. This failed to stop the tide of white settlers, and conflicts continued. But the Tlingits remained independent of the Europeans.

Aleksandr Andreevich Baranov had many troubles. The fur company's ships often failed to arrive with supplies. Grains especially were short because the settlers' attempts to farm had failed.

In the waters off this rugged and reefy California coastal
area lies a common homeland for sea otters, who almost
never go ashore. In a 1970 census, over a thousand otters
were seen along 100 miles of California coast, from
Monterey to Point Conception.

Yankee clipper ships rescued him on many occasions with their cargoes.

On a partnership arrangement with Baranov, the Americans borrowed his natives and took them south to hunt otters. This made hunting easy for the Bostonians and helped Baranov, who had no large ships. Sometimes Baranov's partners set the hunters ashore on a California island and returned months later for the haul of pelts. Another way they collected pelts was to trade with the Indians of California, Oregon, and Washington.

With the Aleutian otter branch pruned back so severely, Baranov often hunted far below Sitka. He risked irritating Great Britain and the United States, whose beaver hunters were putting down roots in Washington and Oregon. However, because his country's relations with Spain were friendly, at first he restrained his greed in the Californias.

In the last quarter of the eighteenth century, Spain claimed that her Californias ran as far as the Arctic. In reality she had no settlements north of San Francisco. She had laws against poaching her furs, but was too busy against Napoleon in Europe to send the colony ships to patrol the California coastline.

Her tiny settlements of San Diego, Los Angeles, Santa Barbara, Monterey, and San Francisco were forbidden to trade with foreign ships, which were allowed only brief stops in port for water and firewood. However, when supply ships from the motherland failed to appear or failed to bring them necessities (and a few luxuries), the colonists would often ignore the law and trade pelts for the goods in the well-stocked holds of the clippers, such as pots, pans, shovels, shoes, food, and yardgoods.

Baranov became more desperate for furs and began to direct occasional forays to pirate the California otter. In a daring action, one of his expeditions plucked 2,300 pelts from under the noses of the San Franciscans. Aleuts portaged over 30 miles of land to the San Francisco Bay. In the shadow of the military garrison they found otters blanketing the shores of the bay and mouths of the streams. It was like early times in Alaska.

Next, Baranov established a settlement in upper California as a base of operations for his hunters and as a farm to supply his Alaskan settlers. Fort Rus is now called Fort Ross.

This fort remained Russian for 29 years and during this time hunters took 50,000 of the 150,000 otters believed to live between Baja California and Alaska. With these and batches of 5,000 annually for 20 more years, the species was nearly extinct by 1900. No lesson was learned from over-harvesting the Alaskan otter.

In 1841, exactly a century after Vitus Bering led the Russians to the new world, they sold Fort Rus to John Sutter. Twenty-six years later Russia sold Alaska to the United States. The end of the Russian visit in the northeast Pacific Ocean was the end of a dramatic and tragic chapter in the history of the sea otter.

The sea otter became nearly extinct, then slowly made a recovery. He was given protection by the 1911 fur treaty between Russia, Japan, England, and the United States. Just before the signing, 28 men in 14 boats brought in a dozen otter pelts, which they sold for $800 each. After that, poaching and a black market continued. On one occasion seven furs brought $3500—and a $5000 fine.

Just before World War II a coast guard cutter found an otter colony at Amchitka Island, at the far end of the Aleutian chain. The United States then laid plans to increase the otter's numbers in order to revive the fur trade with controlled harvesting. Many a serviceman stationed in the Aleutians during World War II discovered and enjoyed "those goofy little animals playing offshore."

In 1945 the otter count was believed to be about 3,000. So successful was the combination of legal protection and wildlife service efforts that the northern otter population flourished enough to allow Alaska to cull its otters for the world fur market in 1968. By 1973, however, otter fur had not proved to be fashionable.

Ten
Evolution and Survival

THE sea otter is an aquatic animal who has made a full circle in his evolution. His ancestors, like those of other land animals, originated in the sea and later moved to the land. Now he is back in the sea.

During the first century of the great hunt men described otters as living in shoals and blackening the shores of California. These reports do not necessarily mean that the animals had left the ocean completely, just that they lived along the shelf or

64

shore. Although the sea otters were more easily hunted in the north and the south, pursuing them in the rugged and rockbound sections of the central California coastline proved more difficult. It is now a rare occasion to see a live otter on the beach. Some of those seen ashore are ill and injured.

Either 30 million years ago (according to some scientists) or 100 million years ago (according to others), some land animals returned to the sea and began to adapt their bodies to become proficient in water. The whale, dolphin, and porpoise, all *Cetaceans,* are streamlined to the point of having no outer ear or surface mammary glands. They have almost no hair. Yet the *Cetacean* has distinct arm and finger bones to prove his ancestors once crawled, walked, or hopped on land. The smooth seal has land animal remnants such as distinct toes in his flippers.

Compared to seals, sea otters are poorly adapted to fast swimming and long submergence. Because sea otters feed on slowly moving intertidal and subtidal animals, they have not had to develop fast swimming or deep diving abilities.

Whales and seals are supplied with insulation against the cold—a layer of blubber to help retain body heat. Both the northern and southern otters have a less dependable means of staying warm— by keeping their skin dry.

Otter fur must be kept full of air pockets. When the thin outer layer of fur is wet and clinging, little blisters of air are trapped among the fibers below.

Sea otters must continually groom their fur to maintain an air blanket which keeps the water from touching the skin. While grooming, they may use forepaws and flippers at the same time. This sea otter presses and rubs her fur with her forepaws.

They are a barrier between the warmth and the cold, like thermal clothing or the fiber glass insulation under the roof of a house. Further indication that only the fine outer layer of fur gets wet is the short time (10 or 15 minutes) needed to dry the surface of the coat on the beach in Alaska's damp climate.

Because blubber provides not only warmth but also a storage pantry of surplus food energy, the lack of this tissue layer is a double handicap. To make his heating system function, the otter must eat about one-fifth of his weight in food every day. If he lived out of the water, so great a number of calories would not be necessary. Air does not rob the body of heat as quickly as water does.

The value of fat as an emergency food shelf is shown by the harp seal. After a two-week period of suckling her baby, the mother can abandon it on an ice floe. Here he will survive on his fat for another two weeks. At the end of this time hunger gnaws, and the young seal falls or steps from the ice in search of nourishment. From then on he is off to shift for himself. A sea otter pup depends on his mother for food for almost a year. Sea otter adults and pups seldom have an opportunity to accumulate fat. A sea otter pup would become chilled and weak and would live for only a few days without its mother's care.

Nature has adapted the otter to survive in a narrow habitat at this time in his evolution. In the north, the maximum depth to which he will dive for food is less than 200 feet. Therefore, swimming from island to island is difficult because deep passes and long distances separate most of them. If he had a layer of blubber, it would provide insulation for the period of travel. Many Alaskan otters, newly weaned or old, have starved when their pods, or colonies, grew too large for their local food supply.

Nature makes up for these handicaps by providing the otter with food for which he does not need to lie in wait, chase, or stalk. It is caught up in the paws, carried to the surface, and eaten. An instant dinner can be gathered from the kelp by collecting turban snails without diving to the bottom.

Easy food-gathering methods allow the otter time for grooming its offspring and itself—which is so important for keeping healthy and warm. The mother also has time to help her pup, who has much to learn of survival techniques. He cannot be left alone in a hollow log or in a nest. An otter mother separates herself from her young for mere minutes at a time.

We live in that era of the sea otter's evolution which finds him handicapped both on land and in the sea. He is so far advanced toward sea life that he is awkward on land, yet he retains more land animal characteristics than marine animal characteristics. Even so, on land he does not resemble the nimble, free, and high-spirited creature he is in the water. His flippers are a drag when he navigates the gravelly islands of the north. His body, a streamlined dart in sea or pool, seems to collapse its contours on land. His confidence seems lost,

An Aleutian sea otter dines on a clam, opened by cracking
the shell against the rock on his chest. Sometimes, if the
otter has more than one clam, he will knock the two together
to open them.

Gulls often wait for the chance to swoop down and pounce on morsels of fish that the sea otter has discarded or missed.

and he shuffles along as though without spirit. To see him like this is to wonder how he could be related to that lightning-quick clown, the river otter.

In 1971 oceanographer Jacques Cousteau produced a television film on California sea otters. It showed how swift and eel-like they travel underwater. Little Esprit, who befriended the Cousteau divers and photographers, resembled a sleek, polished corkscrew as he twisted, turned, and gyrated around them.

Men have described the otter as pear-shaped or as a sack of liquid on island beaches. Perhaps it is the sea otter's coat which makes this picture. It sags. The pelt can be stretched to half again its size, which is a definite advantage in the sea. The otter can pull his loose hide into folds, press water from the surface of these folds with his forepaws, and lap up the excess moisture. He can reach down between his flippers as he floats, grasp some back skin, and pull it toward him for preening.

Other adaptations to the environment have occurred. Teeth developed into crushers for snail and mussel shells, the digestive tract adjusted to the shell fragments swallowed regularly, and kidneys developed into larger organs to accommodate salt water elimination.

Why did the northern otter not go to sea completely like the California otter? Northern Pacific storms are wilder than the southern ones, and northern pods are forced to take refuge ashore. Also, they are farther from large land predators, people, and civilization and so are less harassed.

Eleven

To See an Otter

THERE are few reported social encounters between people and otters. Recently, a member of Friends of the Sea Otter looked up while photographing some underwater scenes and noticed the back of a resting otter. The man rose to the surface and put his arms around the otter, slowly and gently. The otter, just as gently disengaged himself and swam leisurely away.

Only one abalone diver has reported meeting an otter while both were at work in the fisheries. The otter darted head first into a sea cave which was too small to include his tail. With that tail waving before his faceplate the diver could not resist giving it a brisk yank. In a wink the otter popped out of the crevice to face his rival. Both man and otter were so shocked that they took off in different directions.

Not many people have the opportunity to observe this animal from a boat or beach in the Alaskan seas, Prince William Sound, the Pribilof Islands, or the Aleutian Islands. However, California has more than 150 miles of coastline where rafts of otters at work and play might be seen. Their range is from central California north to Monterey Bay. Their refuge, established legally years ago, lies within their range and is about 100 miles in length.

Rafts, or colonies, tend to congregate near Monterey, so this may be the most profitable area for observation. Pacific Grove, the city which entertains the migrating Monarch butterflies each fall, is also a good area. Close to Monterey is Point Lobos State Park whose rangers help many of its annual visitors spot the otters offshore.

The California state highway which runs along the cliffs above the sea and parallels the official otter refuge has road markers that inform motorists of the existence of the refuge. Look for them where kelp fans over the surface of the sea like red-brown lace. Seagulls often rest on swells near feeding otters to pounce on morsels of the otters' food. Field glasses are needed because the otters are usually far from the observer.

During mating the male sea otter grasps the female's nose, often causing it to become swollen and later resulting in scar tissue. After mating, this male and female stayed together to sleep, groom, and eat. Of the two, the female (left) was more cautious about outside intruders.

Just beyond the line of breakers rolling in to shore, the otters will be resting, playing, feeding, and grooming. If the surf is not too noisy, the sound of an otter beating a clam against a rock will carry to the cliff top.

Colonies in both the north and the south present the same picture—a random scattering of objects like short logs with a knob at one end. The "logs" may be cruising about the sprawling kelp, or they may be frolicking with one another in the combers. Some may be napping.

During the middle of the day, these social animals drift together. Sometimes their flippers stand like sails awaiting a breeze. The short forelegs are usually scratching, buffing, and rubbing because the fur's condition is a life or death matter for the otter. Soil may let water pass through the thin outer layer of fur to mat the fluffed fibers beneath. If cold water chills the skin, pneumonia and death can result.

When the wind rises, otters grow excited and caper in the choppy water, churning out wakes of bubbles and tossing foam and froth helter-skelter. Porpoising or leaping can carry them clear of the sea surface. Pinwheeling is another sport—spinning around through the surf with their licorice-black noses pressed against their flippers.

Twice during 1970 Alaskan otters were flown to the coasts of Washington and Oregon to serve as seed for new colonies. The first airplane load of them scattered far and wide when they were released. For this reason, officials held the second load in cages in the sea for a period before freeing them. The shock of unfamiliar territory was eased and these otters remained in the neighborhood.

In California natural extension of the range is slowly taking place.

Young male otters began to roam south of their refuge in the late 1960s. The nucleus of a temporary colony was seen in 1970 near Santa Cruz. Also in that year, a male spent some time in San Diego Bay before heading south toward Baja California

where his ancestors lived until the great hunt eliminated them. According to Judson Vandevere, California sea otter specialist, this roving means that the California population, like the northern population, has individuals that explore. An extended range will provide more space and food.

The chance to see an otter in captivity increases with the steady growth of the Alaskan otter population. Laws are still in effect which fine a poacher one to five thousand dollars and a year in prison for capturing or for killing an otter. But as the population recovers, federal and state governments are more generous in allowing otters to be taken for study.

From 1955 to 1961, Susie lived a healthy, happy life in the Woodland Park Zoo of Seattle, Washington, the only otter of 50 to survive. All the others died soon after capture. Once the state assigned three otters to one of the California marine institutes, but they died within a few weeks or months. At the end of 1970, the last of five otters died in the Woodland Park Zoo.

Gus was the only otter in captivity in 1965 when he arrived at the Tacoma, Washington, aquarium.

Blondy, a captive female, reaches for a piece of fish. She puts the first piece into a chest pouch, which is a loose flap of skin under her arm. Otters often keep food inside these pouches until they can eat it. The otter's flattened hind feet, or flippers, also are clearly visible in this photo.

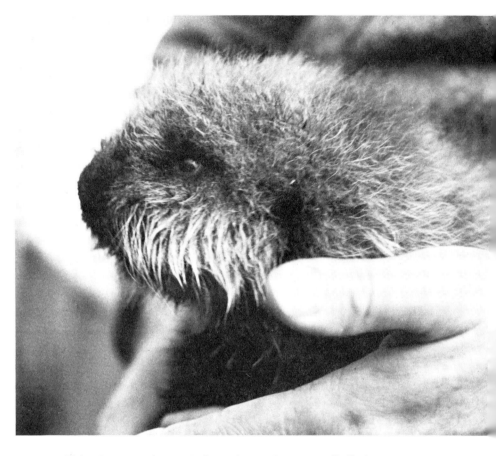

This close-up of a pup's face shows the dense, fluffy fur, which is still very light-colored.

This is a laboratory of sorts because the neighboring Bureau of Sport Fisheries and Wildlife can study the captive otters. After delighting visitors for three years, Gus was finally joined by another male and three females. Chances for survival were improved when they moved into $35,000 quarters in 1969. The new habitat has two salt water pools with constantly changing sea water, and there is no way visitors can endanger the otters by tossing them objects.

To understand the security measures in Tacoma one must understand how unusual the otter is. He is a temperamental creature, highstrung and touchy. His feelings get ruffled easily, and the emotional upset leads to physical stress. He may die as a result. Scientists are studying the few otters in captivity to determine their makeup and the reason for their high death rate. Much remains to be learned about this unique mammal. Until recent years biologists, zoologists, veterinarians, and others have had little opportunity to examine its behavior closely.

It is a challenge for a zoo or aquarium not only to keep an otter healthy in captivity but to keep him fed. His appetite for budget-shattering foods such as clam, squid, octopus, and red snapper in great quantity can make authorities wary of assuming responsibility for him. The zoo director who says the sea otter eats more than a lion and costs more to feed than an elephant may exaggerate very little. Woodland Park Zoo's otter budget was five dollars per day per otter for its family of five.

However, when visitors are enjoying the otters —watching them eat snowballs tossed by their keeper, open a clam, or play porpoise with each other, it must be difficult to remember practical matters like expenses. The otters are too much fun.

Twelve
An Otter Safari

THERE are three reasons why otters are little known and little understood compared with many other animals. First, they are sensitive and cannot be herded or managed but must be treated as individuals.

Second, since 1911 federal law has protected otters. Until recently when the Alaskan otter population swelled, the federal government would not let them be taken for study purposes. The U.S. Bureau of Sport Fisheries and Wildlife had the

Lori and her baby, Smitty, were two of the five Aleutian sea otters that were taken to new lodgings at the Woodland Park Zoo in Seattle.

funds and manpower for experimenting with otter transplants with a view toward colonizing.

Third, the otter's enormous appetite discourages aquariums and zoos. His requirements for clean water and protection also demand a large budget.

However, in November of 1967 a half-dozen adventurous animal lovers received government permission to capture five otters on the beach of an Aleutian island. They wanted to establish an otter family in the Woodland Park Zoo at Seattle. Residents there had enjoyed their first otter, Susie, for six years until she died in 1961.

The hunters prepared themselves by studying all they could find about *Enhydra's* history, behavior, habits, and physical and emotional makeup. They learned that stormy, winter weather was the best time to capture an otter because it seeks shelter on the beach more often and for longer periods. They learned what delicate handling would be necessary for the creature's survival.

In fact, concern for the otter's well-being drove the men to overwork under the severe climatic conditions, and all of them became ill. One man even collapsed on the beach after a week of wading in freezing shallows and creeping over the slippery sea cabbage that coats the rocky shores. But the men refused to be stopped by this or by sleet, rain, high winds, or snow flurries.

There were occasional nips because an excited otter can bite through heavy boots or layers of foul-weather gear. Lori, a mother, fought frantically to escape with her pup. When the youngster became alarmed, she would nurse and cuddle him until he was calm, and then she would begin her struggle again. Instinct to protect her young was so strong and Lori struggled so often to escape with Smitty from the holding tank, that the men feared for the pup's life. Until the otters were enplaned and beyond the scent of their sea and island, Lori refused to surrender and relax. Two men carried each

The Woodland Park otters were kept clean and were well fed.
The keeper cleaned their pool and grotto several times a day.

After their morning swim, the Woodland Park otters would dry and groom themselves.

caged otter across the tundra with the care due a cargo of eggs. After an hour and a half of this travel, the otter was carried by truck to a holding tank.

Once five animals were collected, they were moved in a mattress softened truck to the airport and their cages suspended over canvas in the first-class compartment of an airline jet. To keep the otters from dehydrating during the ten-hour flight, they were splashed with seawater each hour and glass after glass of fresh water was poured directly into their mouths. The cabin temperature was lowered and ice blocks surrounded the cages. Otters cannot be out of the water long without suffering from heat because their systems cannot adjust to temperature change.

Three thousand miles away, the otter family was settled in the Woodland Park Zoo—a female and her nursing pup, an old male, and two other males. The private collecting group had set a record: the otters had arrived alive and more of them had been carried by airplane over a longer distance than in any official project in the past.

The tricky otter safari required the help of a fire department, two airlines, the U.S. Fish and Wildlife Service, the U.S. Atomic Energy Commission, veterinarians, biologists, and the Alaskan government in addition to the labors of the hunters.

This ended the first phase of the effort to bring pleasure to zoo fans and otter admirers. The second phase was to keep them alive. Woodland Park Zoo officials had the benefit of six years' experience with Susie. Alas, none of the new family had Susie's good fortune—the last died in the fall of 1970.

While they lived, the five appeared to be happy and enjoyed the best of everything humans could give them. Several times daily the keepers cleaned the pool and hosed down the grotto to help keep the animals and their lustrous fur unsoiled. After experimenting the zoo veterinarian learned to wheedle the otters into eating their vitamin B$_1$. He would soak the pills overnight inside a chunk of squid to make them into a tasty, pasty wad.

The feeding schedule included a meal at 8:00 A.M., a second breakfast at 11:45 A.M., and a light feeding at 3:00 P.M. Dinner at 3:45 consisted of 30 pounds of octopus, red snapper, shellfish, and squid. Although otters exercise less in captivity, their bodies still need many calories for warmth.

After a morning frolic in the pool the otters would dry and groom themselves in the open or on the woodshavings in the dens. They groomed almost half of their waking hours. A dim floodlight on their grotto made night much like day. The family often spent the night outside. Otters are active at night.

There is no doubt that these otters gave immense and unforgettable pleasure to thousands of men, women, and children. They were sorely missed after 1970.

Thirteen

Otter Enemies

THE otter rises and falls in the sea swells as though held afloat by the leafy arms of the seaweed tree. A moment later he is surfing and leaping clear of the water, porpoising gaily over and through the white-capped combers.

Perhaps the bouncy otter has more time to play because his food is plentiful and he is seldom on the alert against enemies. With enemies like other animals, he might not have survived in the sea, which demands so much of his time to keep healthy and well fed.

There is little proof that the otter is preyed upon by other marine creatures, although two otter carcasses have been found that carried the mark of a shark tooth in them.

The killer whale, *Orca*, on whose feeding path all of the otters live, relishes the sea lion, elephant seal, and fur seal. He is expected to relish the otter, but concrete evidence of this is lacking. Many people have reported the whale spooking the otter but not eating it. A biologist in the Russian Commander Islands saw a herd of whales head toward shore and terrify a colony of otters who bolted to the rocky points and beaches.

Animals other than the shark and whale are more of a nuisance than a threat to the Alaskan otter. The bald eagle is considered an enemy because otter remains have been found in an eagle nest, but otter is probably not a preferred food. An eagle once carried off a live pup, but usually otter pups float alone on the sea while eagles go about their business. The biologist in the Commanders has watched eagles and gulls swoop around feeding otters and later snatch meat from them. Although the otters dived repeatedly to shake off their attackers, their efforts were in vain.

When nature is allowed to take its course, the chain of plant and animal life is subject to checks and balances. Predators, weather, and disease are three of nature's tools for preventing one species in a habitat or ecosystem from growing out of proportion to the others. Winter is a major enemy.

Rough seas prevent easy foraging for food, and high waves can dash an otter against the rock reefs. Winter is especially hazardous for a pup.

In California there is no evidence of starvation among the otters. The slow increase in otter population after 1938, encouraged the otters to gradually extend their range. In order that the otter stay peppy and warm, his system needs a high fuel intake. When he is not diving or vigorously cleaning his fur, the cold water drains away the body heat provided by the food calories.

If a boy or girl weighing 120 pounds had an appetite in proportion to the otter's, he or she would need some 24 pounds of meat a day (perhaps up to 192 hot dogs). An 80-pound otter requires 16 pounds of seafood—close to 5,000 calories.

One place where sea otters come to look for food is in the abalone beds between Cambria and Morro Bay, California. Members of the abalone industry have said that the otters were cutting down the abalone yield. However, conservationists have insisted that the sea otters have not been the only reason for the decline in some of the beds. They also claim that increasing competition among abalone fishermen as well as the fishing done by sportsmen may have accounted for the decreasing yield.

In 1970 a bill was introduced in the California state legislature to allow the taking of otters by individuals other than government officials. Conservationists succeeded in stopping the measure in legislative committee. In 1971, three abalone fishermen who killed a sea otter were fined one thousand dollars each and placed on probation for three years. In 1972 the Federal Marine Mammal Protection Act placed the sea otter under the stewardship of the U.S. government from 1973 on.

Rifles and spearguns also are hazards to the California colony. As late as 1969, 11 carcasses washed ashore near the southern border of the otter range. Official examination of the carcasses revealed these causes of death—gunshot wounds, heavy blows, and deep cuts.

Today's enemy for all life on the planet is pollution of the environment. A threat to life is the increasing incidence of oil well blowouts, spillages from oil tankers, and cleaning of bilges in the off-shore waters. Near the southern tip of the otter refuge (and the red abalone fisheries) at least one tanker daily loads petroleum from a pipeline running into the sea. A ruptured line spilled crude oil here in the late 1960s.

Cities and streams along the California coast drain pesticides, industrial wastes, sewage, harmful bacteria, dry-cleaning solvents, and other chemicals into the ocean. When the polluted water soils the sea otter's fur, it loses its water-repelling quality, and so the sea otter dies. The pollution not only makes the water unclean but also affects the otters' food sources. Often a pesticide stops the spawning of shellfish. Other pollutants spare the adult organism but kill the young.

In 1969 an otter dying on the beach near Monte-

People do not often have an opportunity to see an otter close up. Even in seemingly ideal surroundings in a zoo otters do not live for a very long time. This captive female otter is eating a large codfish head.

rey had nose sores which prevented his diving for food. The nostrils carried bacteria found in human and animal wastes. Otter watchers have found the mammals using discarded cans and pop bottles for anvils.

The latest hazard for the otter is pleasure-boat propellors. This cause of death is more obvious than that from poison in the otter's system.

Unfortunately, no seashore or point on the high seas is spared pollutants. Jacques Cousteau, oceanographer, claims that the seas are more polluted than the land. Thor Heyerdahl confirmed this in 1969 and 1970 when he crossed the Atlantic in his reed boat and found the sea clotted with refuse and filmed with oil.

The sea otter's struggle for survival has been long and bitter. Nature rescued the sea otters in the past by adjusting them to marine life even before they were fitted out completely as a marine species. Today they may be facing adversaries they cannot outwit and to which they are unable to adapt, such as pollution of offshore waters.

The next chapter in the sea otter drama will depend in part on human choices and actions to control the environment and manage resources. In recent times humans have proved to be the sea otter's greatest friends, and so, undoubtedly, humans will continue to ease the struggle and to help the sea otter survive.

Reference List

Atherton, Gertrude F. 1969. *Rezanov*. Reprint of 1906 ed. Boston, Massachusetts: The Gregg Press, Inc.

Barabash-Nikiforov, I. I. 1947. *The Sea Otter (Kalan)*. Soviet Ministrov RSFSR. Translated from Russian by Dr. A. Birron and Z. S. Cole. Israel Program for Scientific Translations.

Boolootian, Richard A. 1969. The Distribution of the California Sea Otter. *California Fish and Game*, vol. 47, no. 3, pp. 287–292.

Buell, Robert K. and Skladal, Charlotte N. 1968. *Sea Otters and the China Trade*. New York: David McKay Company, Inc.

California Department of Fish and Game. 1968. Report on the Sea Otter, Abalone, and Kelp Resources in San Luis Obispo and Monterey Counties and Proposals for Reducing the Conflict Between the Commercial Abalone Industry and the Sea Otter.

Coues, Elliott. 1970. *Fur-Bearing Animals of North America*. Reprint of 1877 ed. New York: Arno Publishing Company.

Cox, Keith W. 1962. California Abalone, Family Haliotidae. *California Fish and Game, Fish Bulletin 118*. pp. 57–60.

94   *The Sea Otter's Struggle*

Daugherty, Anita E. 1966. *Marine Mammals of California.* Sacramento: California Department of Fish and Game.

Ebert, Earl E. 1968. A Food Habits Study of the Southern Sea Otter, *Enhydra Lutris Nereis. California Fish and Game,* vol. 54, no. 1, pp. 33–42.

Fisher, Edna N. 1939. Habits of the Southern Sea Otter. *Journal of Mammalogy,* vol. 20, no. 1, pp. 21–36.

———. 1940. Early Life of a Sea Otter Pup. *Journal of Mammalogy,* vol. 21, no. 2, pp. 132–137.

Hall, K. R. L. and Schaller, G. B. 1964. Tool-Using Behavior of the California Sea Otter. *Journal of Mammalogy,* vol. 45, no. 2, pp. 287–298.

Harris, C. J. 1968. *Otters, a Study of Recent Lutrinae.* London: Weidenfeld and Nicholson.

Kenyon, Karl W. 1959. The Sea Otter. *Smithsonian Report for 1958.* pp. 399–407.

———. 1963. Recovery of a Fur-Bearer. *Natural History Magazine,* vol. 72, no. 9, pp. 12–21.

———. 1969. *The Sea Otter in the Eastern Pacific Ocean.* North American Fauna, Number 68. Washington, D.C.: U.S. Bureau of Sport Fisheries and Wildlife.

———. 1971. Return of the Sea Otter. *National Geographic,* vol. 140, no. 4, pp. 520–39.

Laycock, George. 1968. The Beautiful, Sad Face of Amchitka. *Audubon Magazine,* vol. 70, no. 6, pp. 8–12, 14, 16, 18–20, and 22–25.

Laycock, George, and Laycock, Ellen. 1970. *The Flying Sea Otters.* New York: Grosset and Dunlap, Inc.

Life Magazine. 1965. Uproar Over Otters; a Rare Breed Is Imperiled by a Nuclear Test. Vol. 59, no. 16, pp. 151–152.

Mattison, James A., Jr., and Hubbard, R. C. 1965. Southern Sea Otter. *Pacific Discovery,* vol. 18, no. 6, pp. 16–17.

McCracken, Harold. 1957. *Hunters of the Stormy Sea.* Garden City, New York: Doubleday.

McCutcheon, Steve. 1965. Atomic Blast vs. Sea Otter? *Audubon Magazine,* vol. 67, no. 6, pp. 376–381.

Ogden, Adele. 1941. The California Sea Otter Trade 1784–1848. Berkeley and Los Angeles: University of California Press.

Otter Raft. 1969– . Semi-Annual. Big Sur, California: Friends of the Sea Otter.

Outdoor California. 1958. The Playful Sea Otter. Vol. 19, no. 8, pp. 12–14.

Paca, Lillian G. 1965. *California Sea Otter.* Carmel, California: D'Angelo Publishing Company.

Peattie, D. C. 1961. Return of the Sea Otter. *Reader's Digest,* vol. 78, pp. 121–124.

Ray, Carleton. 1972. The Sea Otter. *Ranger Rick's Nature Magazine,* vol. 6, no. 1.

Ricketts, Edward F., and Calvin, Jack. 1968. *Between Pacific Tides, Fourth Edition.* Joel W. Hedgepeth, ed. Stanford, California: Stanford University Press.

Roth, Hal. 1971. Sea Otter Population Now Booming Modestly in Western Waters. *Smithsonian,* vol. 1, no. 12, pp. 30–37.

Seed, Alice, compiler. 1972. *Sea Otter in Eastern North Pacific Waters.* Seattle, Washington: Pacific Search Books.

Stoutenburg, Adrien, 1968. *Animals at Bay.* Garden City, New York: Doubleday.

Sunset Magazine. 1965. How to See the Sea Otter. Vol. 136, pp. 51–54.

Vandevere, Judson E., and Mattison, James A., Jr. 1970. Sea Otters. *Sierra Club Bulletin,* Vol. 55, no. 10. pp. 12–15.

Vincenzi, F. 1962. The Sea Otter at Woodland Park Zoo. *Interzoo Yearbook for 1961,* vol. 3. London: Hutchinson.

Von Langsdorff, Georg H. 1968. *Voyages and Travels in Various Parts of the World.* Boston, Massachusetts: The Gregg Press, Inc.

X